How to use this book

Follow the advice, in italics, given for you on each page.
Support the children as they read the text that is shaded in cream.
***Praise** the children at every step!*

Detailed guidance is provided in the Read Write Inc. Phonics Handbook

8 reading activities

Children:
- *Practise reading the speed sounds.*
- *Read the green and red words for the story.*
- *Listen as you read the introduction.*
- *Discuss the vocabulary check with you.*
- *Read the story.*
- *Re-read the story and discuss the 'questions to talk about'.*
- *Re-read the story with fluency and expression.*
- *Practise reading the speed words.*

Speed sounds

Consonants   *Say the pure sounds (do not add 'uh').*

f ⓕⓕ	l ll	m mm	n nn kn	r rr	s ss ⓒⓔ ⓢⓔ	v ve	z zz s	sh	ⓣⓗ	ng ⓝⓚ

b bb	c k ck	d dd	g gg	h	j	p pp	qu	t tt	w wh	x	y	ch tch

Vowels   *Say the sounds in and out of order.*

at	hen head	in	on	up	day	see happy	high	blow

zoo	look	car	for door snore	fair	whirl	shout	boy

*Each box contains one sound but sometimes more than one grapheme. Focus graphemes are **circled**.*

Green words

p<u>i</u><u>nk</u>   s<u>i</u><u>nk</u>   l<u>oo</u>k

m<u>ou</u><u>se</u>   h<u>ou</u><u>se</u>   sn<u>ou</u>t   <u>ou</u><u>ch</u>   p<u>ou</u><u>nce</u>   <u>sh</u><u>ou</u>t

r<u>ou</u>nd   sp<u>ou</u>t   <u>ou</u>t

wi<u>th</u>`<u>ou</u>t  →  wi<u>th</u> <u>ou</u>t       a`b<u>ou</u>t → ab<u>ou</u>t

sni<u>ff</u> → sni<u>ff</u>ly

Red words

want   <u>the</u>   my   do   to

Vocabulary check

Discuss the meaning (as used in the story) after the children have read each word.

	definition:
spout	*the place where the tea pours from a teapot*
pounce	*jump*
snout	*a mouse's nose*

Punctuation to note in this story:

Get Look It A	*Capital letters that start sentences*
.	*Full stop at the end of each sentence*
!	*Exclamation mark used to show anger*
.....	*Wait and see*

Look out!

Introduction

Do you know anyone who has ever had a mouse in their house - not a pet mouse, but a wild mouse? What do you think people think about this? One day, the family in this story find a mouse as it runs about their house.

Will it run out?

Story written by Gill Munton
Illustrated by Tim Archbold

Look out! Look out!

I can see a mouse about!

A mouse with pink feet

and a sniffly snout!

Puss wants to pounce,

and Mum wants to shout!

Ouch!

Look out! Look out!

I can see a mouse about!

Look out! Look out!

I can see a mouse about!

It runs round the sink

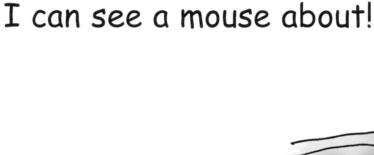

and it runs up the spout -

A mouse in my house! Get out! Get out!

Look out! Look out!

I can see a mouse about!

Look out! Look out!

I can see a mouse about!

A mouse in my house

I can do without!

It runs in, it runs round -

and then it runs out!

Look out! Look out!

I can see a mouse about!

Questions to talk about

Re-read the page. Read the question to the children. Tell them whether it is a **FIND IT** *question or* **PROVE IT** *question.*

FIND IT

✔ *Turn to the page*

✔ *Read the question*

✔ *Find the answer*

PROVE IT

✔ *Turn to the page*

✔ *Read the question*

✔ *Find your evidence*

✔ *Explain why*

Page 8:   FIND IT   *What does the mouse look like?*
What does Puss want to do?
What does Mum want to do?

Page 9:   PROVE IT   *What does the mouse do now?*

Page 10:   FIND IT   *Where does the mouse go?*

Page 13:   PROVE IT   *Do you think the mouse comes to visit again?*